HOW TO EMBRACE
POSITIVE
TRANSFORMATION

Master the Art of Communication, Learn to Celebrate Diversity, Remain Open to Change, and Build a Legacy

by

MAHUYA GUPTA

Copyright © 2024 by Mahuya Gupta

All rights reserved. No part of this book may be reproduced in any form without permission in writing from the author.

No part of this publication may be reproduced or transmitted in any form or by any means, mechanical or electronic, including photocopying or recording, by any information storage and retrieval system, or by email or any other means whatsoever without permission in writing from the author.

TABLE OF CONTENTS

Introduction 7

Introduction to New Challenges 11

    Reflections on the Past 11

    The Evolving Mission 11

    The Call to Harmony 12

    Formation of Harmony Teams 12

    Training in Harmony Techniques 12

    Initial Challenges and Adaptation 13

    Cultural Integration 13

    Building Sustainable Alliances 13

    Internal Harmony 14

    Navigating Environmental Challenges 14

    Climax: The Symphony of Harmony 15

The Call to Harmony 17

    A Changing Symphony 17

    Discovering the Harmony Stones 17

    The Four Harmonic Realms 18

    Forming Harmony Teams 19

    Training in Harmony Techniques 19

Initiation Ritual: Harmonic Convergence 20

Initial Challenges in Harmonic Realms 20

The Resonance of Harmony in Diverse Settings 22

The Challenges of Skepticism and Resistance 23

Culmination in a Harmonic Festival 23

Conclusion: Echoes of Harmony 24

The Call to Harmony – Summary with Leadership Lessons 27

Formation of Harmony Teams 31

Understanding the Four Harmonic Realms 31

Defining Harmony Teams 31

The Importance of Diversity 31

Selecting the Teams 32

Forming the Teams 32

Training the Teams 33

Facing Initial Challenges 33

Dealing with Skepticism 33

Showcasing Success 34

Reflecting and Planning for the Future 34

Conclusion: Ongoing Journey 34

Formation of Harmony teams - Management and Leadership Lessons 35

Training in Harmony Techniques 39

    The Sanctum of Wisdom 39

Training in Harmony Techniques – Summary with Leadership Lessons 47

Initial Challenges and Adaptation & Cultural Integration 51

Building Sustainable Alliances 61

Navigating Environmental Challenges 69

Climax - The Symphony of Harmony 79

Conclusion: Embracing Positive Transformation .. 83

Disclaimer 85

About the Author 87

May I Ask You For A Small Favor? 89

Other Books Written By The Author 91

Introduction

Book 1, "Harness the Power of Positivity," follows the Luminary leaders as they find a hidden library filled with ancient knowledge and cosmic wisdom. The Luminaries, each representing a different aspect of harmony, are guided by Aria, their celestial mentor. Aria introduces them to their mission: to spread harmony and positive change throughout the universe.

The Luminaries go on a journey to learn the principles of harmony and positive thinking. They face challenges that teach them the power of positive thinking and working together.

- The Luminary of Physical Harmony learns to heal ecosystems, rejuvenating damaged environments. This Luminary's journey highlights the need for balance and vitality in the physical world.

- The Luminary of Emotional Harmony explores the emotional landscapes of the cosmos, finding ways to bring comfort and stability to emotionally troubled places. This Luminary's path shows the impact of empathy and emotional intelligence in fostering harmony.

- The Luminary of Social Harmony works to bridge societal divides, encouraging unity in regions troubled by conflict and resource scarcity. This Luminary's story emphasizes the importance of collaboration and mutual understanding in creating cohesive communities.

- The Luminary of Environmental Harmony focuses on preserving biodiversity and creating sustainable ecosystems. This Luminary's journey shows the need for harmony between humanity and the environment to ensure a balanced and sustainable future.

As the Luminaries learn from their challenges and grow into their roles as cosmic leaders, they come together in a grand Symphony of Harmony, demonstrating the culmination of their efforts. This cosmic event becomes a ray of hope, signalling the positive changes they have started in the universe.

Key Themes from Book 1:

- The transformative power of positive thinking and harmony.

- The importance of collaboration and empathy in overcoming challenges.

- The balance between physical, emotional, social, and environmental harmony.

- The value of spreading positive change to create a better future for all cosmic beings.

The book ends with the Luminary leaders ready for the next phase of their journey, having ignited the spark of harmony. With the hidden library as their base, they are prepared to explore new realms, face new challenges, and continue their mission of spreading positive change and harmony across the cosmos. This sets the stage for Book 2, where the Luminaries will build on their experiences and take on a broader mission to spread harmony in diverse environments.

Introduction to New Challenges

After successfully spreading positive energy, the Luminaries now face a new adventure. Their past achievements and the wisdom they've gained stay with them as they gather in the hidden library. Aria, their guide, feels a change in the cosmic energies, signaling new challenges ahead.

Reflections on the Past

The chapter starts with the Luminaries reflecting on their past quest. Each one shares their experiences, the cities they visited, the people they influenced, and the challenges they faced. This sharing session helps them combine their individual experiences into a shared understanding.

Aria, with her calm presence, leads the discussion. She encourages the Luminaries to think deeply about the positive impact they've had. Through a series of stories, they recall encounters with skeptics, the transformation of communities, and the spirit that helped them succeed.

The Evolving Mission

As they share their stories, Aria points out the importance of the positive changes they've started. She hints that their mission is evolving and now needs a more complex approach. The hidden library, once a place for positive thinking, now feels ready for new challenges, urging the Luminaries to move beyond just joy and optimism.

"A new calling is coming," Aria says, her voice filled with both challenge and opportunity. The Luminaries, sensitive to these changes, listen closely as she describes the next phase of their journey—a journey into the deeper aspects of harmony.

The Call to Harmony

Aria explains this new mission of harmony, which goes beyond simple positivity. She speaks of a world needing balance and unity. Aria introduces Harmony Stones, ancient artifacts that help achieve equilibrium. The Luminaries, curious and eager, learn about this new task—spreading harmony across different places.

Formation of Harmony Teams

With this new mission, Aria guides the Luminaries to form specialized Harmony Teams. Each team focuses on a specific aspect of harmony, matching the strengths and interests of its members. The chapter explores how these teams are formed and the importance of diversity within them.

Aria emphasizes that true harmony comes from the interplay of different talents and perspectives. Each Luminary finds their role in a team, realizing how their unique strengths contribute to positive change in various ways.

Training in Harmony Techniques

As the teams come together, the hidden library becomes a vibrant academy. The Luminaries train intensively, learning not just about positive thinking but also about fostering balance and understanding in different environments.

Aria teaches them how to use the Harmony Stones. The focus is on collective harmony, where every Luminary's effort combines into a powerful force for positive change.

Initial Challenges and Adaptation

The Luminaries soon face initial challenges that test their harmony techniques. They travel to different places, from busy cities to peaceful landscapes, where they encounter obstacles that require creative solutions.

They adapt their training to each unique environment, blending positive thinking with the nuances of harmony. These challenges help the Harmony Teams refine their techniques and adjust to ever-changing situations.

Cultural Integration

A key part of their mission is understanding and respecting different cultures. Each city presents its own traditions, beliefs, and practices. Aria guides the Luminaries to see the importance of cultural nuances in achieving harmony.

The Luminaries learn to harmonize with the cultural practices of each community they visit, making their journey transformative for both themselves and the communities they touch.

Building Sustainable Alliances

As they progress, the Luminaries focus on building sustainable alliances with local communities, organizations, and influencers. The goal is not just immediate change but lasting partnerships that continue to promote harmony.

Positive collaboration is crucial, and Aria ensures these alliances are based on a shared vision of harmony. The narrative explores the careful work of cooperation, negotiation, and understanding needed to build lasting partnerships.

Internal Harmony

Alongside external challenges, the Luminaries also focus on their internal growth. They explore personal balance and peace, guided by Aria's mentorship. This introspective phase shows that their mission is also about personal discovery and self-mastery.

The Luminaries face their own struggles, finding strength in their inner harmony to better contribute to the world. Aria's teachings guide them through self-discovery and personal growth.

Navigating Environmental Challenges

The Luminaries also address environmental challenges that require both positive thinking and an understanding of ecosystem balance. Aria's teachings help them navigate these issues, showing the interconnectedness of positive thinking, harmony, and environmental sustainability.

They become stewards of nature, recognizing that true harmony includes the natural world.

Climax: The Symphony of Harmony

The chapter builds to a climax with a grand event—the Symphony of Harmony. This event symbolizes the culmination of their efforts. The places they've visited, the challenges they've faced, and the alliances they've built come together in a powerful moment of harmony.

The Symphony of Harmony celebrates the unity, balance, and lasting impact of their mission. It shows the tangible results of their collective efforts, resonating through the hearts of those they've helped.

As the Luminaries prepare for their next adventure, the hidden library is filled with anticipation. The chapter ends with a sense of closure and a hint of new beginnings, inviting the reader to continue the journey with the Luminaries.

The Call to Harmony

In the hidden library, surrounded by the soft glow of ancient manuscripts and the hum of cosmic energies, the Luminaries reunited. After their success in spreading positive energy, they stood together, focusing on Aria, their wise guide. Although the echoes of their past mission lingered, Aria's presence now hinted at a new adventure calling them.

A Changing Symphony

Aria began to speak, her voice filling the library with ancient wisdom. She praised their success with positive thinking but suggested it was time to move beyond simple joy and optimism. The cosmic symphony, once tuned to positivity, now called the Luminaries to explore the deeper melodies of harmony.

"The universe," Aria said, looking at each Luminary, "is a grand symphony of energies, each playing its part. Our task now is to tune ourselves to the harmonies beyond positive thinking."

Discovering the Harmony Stones

Aria walked to a sacred pedestal in the center of the library. On it were ancient artifacts—Harmony Stones. These stones glowed softly, syncing with cosmic rhythms and reflecting the intricate dance of energies within them.

"These stones," Aria explained, holding one reverently, "are keys to realms of harmony. Each stone embodies balance and can help us achieve harmony in various environments."

As Aria spoke, the stones hummed gently, and the Luminaries felt their vibrations. These ancient relics promised a deeper understanding of balance, transcending individual joy to embrace the interconnected dance of the universe.

The Four Harmonic Realms

Aria pointed to a cosmic tapestry on the library walls, depicting the Four Harmonic Realms: Physical Harmony, Emotional Harmony, Social Harmony, and Environmental Harmony. Each realm represented a facet of balance crucial for fostering harmony in different settings.

1. **Physical Harmony**: Balancing body and mind, promoting well-being and vitality.

2. **Emotional Harmony**: Creating a positive emotional environment within and around oneself.

3. **Social Harmony**: Balancing relationships, communities, and societal structures for collective well-being.

4. **Environmental Harmony**: Harmonizing humanity's relationship with the natural world, recognizing the interconnectedness of all living things.

"The call to harmony goes beyond positive thinking," Aria said. "It asks us to explore these four realms, understanding that balance is not a single note but a harmonious chord woven through existence."

Forming Harmony Teams

With the Four Harmonic Realms revealed, Aria guided the Luminaries in forming specialized Harmony Teams. Each team would explore a specific realm, uncovering its secrets and spreading harmony. This marked a shift from focusing solely on positive thinking to embracing diverse aspects of balance.

"Your teams should be as diverse as the realms you explore," Aria emphasized. "In diversity, you will find the strength to uncover the melodies of harmony. Each Luminary should align with a realm where they feel most connected."

The Luminaries formed their teams, feeling the cosmic energies align with their chosen realms. The library, now buzzing with the energy of purposeful alignment, became a hub for exploring harmony.

Training in Harmony Techniques

The journey into harmony began with intensive training sessions. The library, once focused on positive thinking, transformed into an academy for studying equilibrium. Aria, guiding this new symphony, taught techniques beyond conventional positivity.

Training covered a wide range of practices, from mindfulness exercises for physical harmony to empathetic communication for emotional harmony. Social harmony was explored through community-building, while environmental harmony focused on eco-conscious practices. Each Luminary, guided by Aria, immersed themselves in their training, discovering the depth of their chosen realm.

"The techniques you learn are not just tools; they are the notes that create the melody of harmony," Aria said. "Let the wisdom of the Four Harmonic Realms guide you as you seek balance."

Initiation Ritual: Harmonic Convergence

As training peaked, Aria led a grand initiation ritual—the Harmonic Convergence. The Luminaries, now skilled in their realms, gathered in a sacred circle. The Harmony Stones at the center glowed, resonating with the Four Harmonic Realms.

Aria, at the heart of the circle, invoked ancient incantations to summon equilibrium. The Luminaries channeled their energy toward the center, creating a collective field of harmony. The room became a sanctuary of convergence, blending the individual notes of each Luminary into a harmonious chord.

"The Harmonic Convergence marks the start of our mission," Aria announced. "Let the harmony guide your actions. You are now guardians of balance, and your journey will echo through the cosmic symphony."

Initial Challenges in Harmonic Realms

Armed with their new skills and the resonance of the Harmonic Convergence, the Harmony Teams set out. Each team explored the realms of physical, emotional, social, and environmental harmony, ready to face their challenges.

In Physical Harmony, the Luminaries explored the balance of body and mind. Mindfulness, holistic well-being, and understanding body rhythms became their focus. They engaged in activities promoting individual well-being and communal understanding of physical health.

In Emotional Harmony, they delved into emotions. Empathy, compassion, and creating positive emotional spaces were key. They worked with individuals and communities to foster emotional well-being, recognizing its impact on collective harmony.

In Social Harmony, they tackled relationships, communities, and societal structures. They focused on community-building, inclusivity, and addressing social disparities. True social harmony was about creating a societal framework promoting equity and well-being for all.

In Environmental Harmony, they faced challenges in balancing humanity with nature. Eco-conscious practices, sustainable living, and preserving biodiversity were central. They worked with communities to promote environmental stewardship, understanding the link between human well-being and a healthy planet.

As they navigated these challenges, they saw the interconnectedness of the Four Harmonic Realms. Aria's teachings guided them to see that true balance extended beyond individual realms, creating a harmonious symphony in various settings.

The Resonance of Harmony in Diverse Settings

The Harmony Teams traveled to diverse cities, each with unique challenges and opportunities. From bustling urban areas to serene natural environments, they adapted their harmony techniques to each setting's specific needs.

In urban areas, they fostered social harmony by bridging community gaps, promoting inclusivity, and addressing societal challenges. They organized events celebrating diversity, encouraging dialogue and understanding among different backgrounds.

In natural settings, they focused on environmental harmony, working with locals to implement sustainable practices, protect ecosystems, and raise awareness about the interconnectedness of human well-being and the planet's health.

Emotional Harmony found expression in schools, healthcare facilities, and community centers. They initiated programs promoting emotional well-being, mindfulness, and mental health awareness.

For Physical Harmony, they adapted well-being practices to each community's needs, organizing fitness programs and providing holistic healthcare access, recognizing the importance of tailoring efforts to unique rhythms.

As they moved from city to city, the resonance of harmony became clear. Communities felt the transformative power of balance, and the Luminaries saw the positive impact of their mission taking root.

The Challenges of Skepticism and Resistance

Despite positive changes, the Luminaries faced skepticism from those doubting their methods. In diverse settings, some resisted, questioning if harmony was possible in a complex world.

Aria's teachings fortified the Luminaries against skepticism. They engaged in open dialogues, addressing concerns, and sharing tangible results. The Harmony Teams navigated skepticism, seeing it as an opportunity to foster understanding and showcase harmony's real-world impact.

Skepticism pushed the Luminaries to refine their communication strategies, emphasizing evidence-based success stories. They realized they needed to demonstrate harmony's effectiveness and break down barriers of doubt.

Culmination in a Harmonic Festival

The narrative built towards a grand culmination—a Harmonic Festival bringing together communities, skeptics, and supporters. The festival celebrated harmony's transformative power, showcasing positive changes in the cities the Luminaries touched.

In a city square filled with vibrant colors and harmonious melodies, the Luminaries saw diverse communities come together. Skeptics who once doubted now experienced harmony's tangible impact. The festival became a testament to the Luminaries' mission, transcending skepticism and spreading positive change.

The Harmonic Festival featured sustainable practices, artistic expressions of emotional harmony, community-building initiatives, and environmental conservation efforts. The Luminaries, alongside the communities they touched, realized that the call to harmony had become a universal melody resonating through diverse settings.

Conclusion: Echoes of Harmony

As the Harmonic Festival ended, Aria addressed the crowd with words echoing through everyone's hearts. The Harmony Teams' journey had unleashed harmony in diverse settings and sparked a global movement.

"The call to harmony," Aria declared, "is not a one-time mission but a continuous symphony echoing through the cosmos. Your efforts prove that harmony is real and can transform communities, bridge divides, and create a balanced, united world."

The Luminaries knew their mission was far from over. The call to harmony had ignited a flame that would keep spreading, transcending boundaries and resonating in the hearts of those yearning for a balanced world.

As the hidden library embraced the festival's fading echoes, the Luminaries prepared for the next phase of their journey. The call to harmony had transformed them, uniting them in a shared purpose that echoed through the cosmic symphony, promising a future where harmony would endure and the Luminaries would continue spreading balance.

The Call to Harmony - Summary with Leadership Lessons

Chapter 2 of the book focuses on the Luminaries answering a new call to spread harmony in various settings. Aria introduces Harmony Stones and guides the Luminaries in forming Harmony Teams dedicated to specific realms of balance. As they face challenges, skepticism, and celebrate success in a Harmonic Festival, key leadership lessons emerge:

1. **Adaptability and Resilience**

- Leaders must be adaptable and resilient, embracing change and uncertainty with a positive mindset and seeing challenges as growth opportunities.

2. **Visionary Leadership**

- Leaders should articulate a compelling vision beyond immediate goals, inspiring their teams to embark on transformative journeys with a shared purpose.

3. **Inclusivity and Diversity**

- Embrace diversity within teams for a holistic perspective, recognizing that varied strengths contribute to a harmonious outcome.

4. **Training and Skill Development**

- Continuous skill development is crucial. Leaders should invest in training and fostering a culture of continuous learning and adaptation.

5. **Cultivating Harmony within Teams**

- Promote a positive team culture, encouraging collaboration, open communication, and a shared commitment to the mission.

6. **Navigating Skepticism with Positive Communication**

- Address skepticism with evidence-based communication, demonstrating the tangible impact of initiatives.

7. **Celebrating Success and Showcasing Impact**

- Create opportunities to celebrate achievements, reinforcing a positive culture and inspiring teams to overcome future challenges.

8. **Global Movement and Long-term Vision**

- Foster a long-term vision, recognizing that positive change is an ongoing journey requiring sustained effort.

9. **Transformational Leadership**

- Prioritize personal growth and inspire teams to evolve, contributing to the collective success of the organization.

10. Positive Thinking as a Catalyst

- Cultivate a positive mindset as a driving force to inspire teams, overcome obstacles, and achieve meaningful results.

Chapter 2 provides leadership insights into the interplay between positive thinking, adaptability, visionary leadership, and creating a harmonious organizational culture. The Luminaries' journey serves as a metaphor for effective leadership in a world where harmony requires continuous innovation, resilience, and a commitment to positive change.

Formation of Harmony Teams

After answering the Call to Harmony, the hidden library filled with a powerful energy. The Luminaries, ready for their next step, began the journey of forming Harmony Teams. Aria, their wise guide, stood among them, ready to explain this new phase.

Understanding the Four Harmonic Realms

In their gathering space, Aria showed the Luminaries a cosmic map highlighting the Four Harmonic Realms: Physical, Emotional, Social, and Environmental Harmony. Each realm had its own unique energy. Aria explained that forming these specialized teams wasn't just an organizational task—it was like creating a cosmic symphony where each person contributed their unique talents.

Defining Harmony Teams

Aria explained that each Luminary would join a team focused on one of the four realms. These teams would work on solving problems, spreading positive changes, and using positive thinking to tackle challenges. The goal was to bring balance to different aspects of life, creating a harmonious impact.

The Importance of Diversity

Aria stressed that diversity within the teams was crucial. Each Luminary had different strengths and perspectives, making the teams stronger. She compared this to the universe thriving on the interaction of different elements.

Selecting the Teams

Aria led the Luminaries through a selection process using Harmony Stones, each representing a different realm. Each Luminary was drawn to a stone that matched their strengths, aligning them with the realm they would focus on.

Forming the Teams

1. **Physical Harmony Team**

- These Luminaries, drawn to the Stone of Vitality, focused on well-being and vitality. The team included experts in fitness, nutrition, mindfulness, and holistic health.

2. **Emotional Harmony Team**

- Guided by the Stone of Compassion, this team aimed to create a symphony of positive emotions. It included counselors, psychologists, artists, and others skilled in understanding human emotions.

3. **Social Harmony Team**

- The Stone of Unity called those dedicated to building strong communities. This team had community organizers, sociologists, activists, and those passionate about social justice.

4. **Environmental Harmony Team**
   - Drawn to the Stone of Stewardship, these Luminaries focused on environmental balance. The team included ecologists, conservationists, and sustainability experts.

Training the Teams

After forming the teams, the hidden library became a training ground. Aria guided each team through practices and techniques related to their specific realm. The Physical Harmony Team explored well-being practices, the Emotional Harmony Team focused on empathy and compassion, the Social Harmony Team worked on community-building, and the Environmental Harmony Team learned about sustainability and eco-conscious practices.

Facing Initial Challenges

Once trained, the teams faced their first challenges. Each team had to adapt their strategies to the unique issues within their realms. They used Aria's teachings and their training to overcome obstacles and demonstrate the benefits of their work.

Dealing with Skepticism

As they began their work, the teams encountered skepticism. Communities were unsure about these new approaches. The Luminary leaders used positive communication and evidence-based results to address concerns and prove the effectiveness of their methods.

Showcasing Success

The culmination of their efforts was a Harmonic Showcase, where the teams demonstrated their successes. Each team presented their achievements, proving the positive impact of their work. This event helped to convert skeptics and celebrate the teams' hard work.

Reflecting and Planning for the Future

After the showcase, the teams reflected on their experiences. They shared insights, challenges, and lessons learned. Aria encouraged them to continue adapting and improving their strategies. She introduced the next phase of their mission: spreading their positive impact to new areas.

Conclusion: Ongoing Journey

With new goals ahead, the Luminaries prepared to continue their work. Guided by Aria's wisdom, they were ready to spread harmony further, using positive thinking to create lasting change.

Formation of Harmony teams - Management and Leadership Lessons

This chapter of the book delves into the intricate process of forming specialized Harmony Teams within the Luminaries, each dedicated to a unique aspect of spreading harmony. As the Luminaries align with the Four Harmonic Realms—Physical, Emotional, Social, and Environmental Harmony—the chapter unfolds the cosmic dance of team formation, emphasizing the importance of diversity. Here are management and leadership lessons derived from the Formation of Harmony Teams:

1. **Vision and Alignment:**

- Effective leaders articulate a compelling vision that aligns with the collective purpose of their teams. Aria's cosmic vision guides the Luminaries, emphasizing the importance of aligning individual strengths with overarching goals.

2. **The Power of Diversity:**

- Diversity is not just a buzzword but a strength. Leaders should recognize the unique contributions of individuals within diverse teams, fostering an environment where varied perspectives and skills amplify the overall effectiveness of the team.

3. **Purpose-Driven Team Formation:**

- Leaders should form teams with a clear purpose, aligning each team with specific realms of expertise. Purpose-driven teams foster a sense of belonging and dedication among team members, contributing to the overall success of the organization.

4. **Selection Processes and Strengths-Based Leadership:**

- The selection ritual highlights the importance of recognizing and leveraging individual strengths. Leaders should adopt strengths-based leadership, aligning team members with tasks that capitalize on their innate abilities and inclinations.

5. **Collaboration and Team Dynamics:**

- Leaders should facilitate an environment where diverse talents come together harmoniously, ensuring that each team member's strengths contribute to the overall success of the team.

6. **Training Grounds for Holistic Development:**

- The hidden library transforms into a training ground, emphasizing the importance of continuous learning. Leaders should provide opportunities for skill development and holistic training, fostering a culture of growth and adaptability within their teams.

7. **Adaptation to Unique Challenges:**

- Leaders must guide their teams in adapting positive thinking techniques to the unique challenges within their chosen realms. The Luminary leaders demonstrate the importance of flexibility and innovation in overcoming obstacles and achieving transformative results.

8. **Navigating Scepticism with Positive Communication:**

- Leaders face scepticism and resistance, and effective communication is key. The Luminary leaders navigate scepticism by employing positive communication strategies, emphasizing evidence-based success stories, and dismantling barriers through open dialogue.

9. **Resilience and Innovation in Leadership:**

- The challenges faced by the Harmony Teams become opportunities for resilience and innovation. Leaders should instil a mindset of resilience, encouraging their teams to adapt and innovate in the face of adversity, reinforcing the transformative potential of positive thinking.

10. **Culmination and Celebration of Success:**

- The Harmonic Showcase becomes a celebration of success, showcasing the tangible impact of the teams' initiatives. Leaders should create platforms to celebrate achievements, fostering a positive culture and inspiring teams to overcome future challenges.

11. Reflection and Continuous Improvement:

- Reflection is crucial for continuous improvement. Leaders, like the Luminary leaders reflecting on their journey, should encourage introspection within their teams, acknowledging successes, learning from challenges, and adapting strategies for ongoing growth.

12. Vision for Future Endeavours:

- Leaders should have a vision for the future, guiding their teams toward new horizons. Aria's Harmonic Vision represents the importance of long-term goals, inspiring teams to envision and work towards a future where positive change is a continuous journey.

In essence, Chapter 3 intertwines wisdom with practical management and leadership lessons. The Formation of Harmony Teams emphasizes the significance of aligning individual strengths, fostering diversity, and guiding teams to adapt positive thinking techniques to the unique challenges they encounter. As the Luminary leaders embark on their cosmic journey, these lessons serve as a compass for leaders in the real world, driving positive change and fostering a culture of continuous improvement and harmonious collaboration.

Training in Harmony Techniques

As the Luminaries continued their journey, forming Harmony Teams became a key step. Inside the hidden library, Luminary leaders and their teams began an important phase—Training in Harmony Techniques. Aria, the timeless guide, once again took center stage to reveal the secrets of cosmic balance.

The Sanctum of Wisdom

The training took place in the sanctum of wisdom, where ancient scrolls shared stories of cosmic harmony. Aria, surrounded by the Luminary leaders and their teams, started teaching how to combine positive thinking with specific strategies to create unity and balance.

"Harmony is not just an idea; it's a living force throughout the universe," Aria said. "In these sessions, you will explore cosmic wisdom, learning techniques that go beyond regular positive thinking. Each strategy is like a thread that weaves into the fabric of harmony."

1. Physical Harmony Techniques: The Dance of Well-being

The Luminary of Physical Harmony led the first session, guiding the team through practices that balanced body and mind.

Positive Thinking Integration:

- **Affirmations of Holistic Wellness:** Leaders practiced affirmations focusing on overall well-being, recognizing the connection between physical and mental health.

Unity and Balance Strategies:

- **Community Well-being Initiatives:** The Luminary encouraged working with local leaders, healthcare providers, and fitness experts to create programs that fit different communities.

2. Emotional Harmony Techniques: Crafting the Symphony of Emotions

The Luminary of Emotional Harmony led the second session, teaching the team how to manage emotions with compassion.

Positive Thinking Integration:

- **Affirmations for Emotional Resilience:** Leaders practiced affirmations that built emotional strength, helping individuals face challenges with grace.

Unity and Balance Strategies:

- **Emotional Well-being Workshops:** The Luminary suggested creating workshops that used creative expression to promote emotional health and allow diverse emotions to coexist peacefully.

3. **Social Harmony Techniques: Weaving the Fabric of Community**

The Luminary of Social Harmony led the third session, focusing on building community unity and inclusivity.

Positive Thinking Integration:

- **Positive Communication for Unity:** Leaders practiced techniques to promote open dialogue and diplomacy, bridging divides within communities.

Unity and Balance Strategies:

- **Inclusive Community Events:** The Luminary inspired organizing multicultural festivals and events to celebrate diversity and strengthen community ties.

4. **Environmental Harmony Techniques: Guardians of Cosmic Balance**

The Luminary of Environmental Harmony led the fourth session, emphasizing the importance of eco-conscious living.

Positive Thinking Integration:

- **Affirmations for Eco-Conscious Living:** Leaders practiced affirmations highlighting the positive effects of eco-friendly habits, understanding the connection between humans and nature.

Unity and Balance Strategies:

- **Sustainable Living Campaigns:** The Luminary motivated the team to launch campaigns promoting sustainable practices and their benefits to community well-being.

5. Cosmic Integration: The Harmony Convergence Ritual

As the sessions progressed, a sense of cosmic energy grew. This led to the Harmony Convergence Ritual, a ceremony that brought together the teachings of physical, emotional, social, and environmental harmony.

In the cosmic chamber, each Luminary leader joined with the energy they had cultivated. Aria guided them through a ceremony that combined positive thinking techniques with strategies for unity and balance.

Harmony Affirmations:

- The leaders recited harmony affirmations together, each infusing positive energy into the ritual. These affirmations reflected physical, emotional, social, and environmental well-being.

Cosmic Integration Symbol:

- They created a mandala symbolizing the interconnectedness of the Four Harmonic Realms, reinforcing the unity and balance of harmony.

Unity Meditation:

- Aria led a meditation merging the positive energy of each Luminary, creating a harmonious symphony of their combined efforts.

As the ritual concluded, the library filled with the energy of unity and balance. Aria saw that the Luminary leaders had become cosmic architects of positive change.

6. Reflection: Embracing Growth and Insights

After the ritual, the leaders gathered to reflect. Aria encouraged them to share their experiences and the energy they had harnessed.

Insights from Physical Harmony:

- The Luminary of Physical Harmony spoke about the power of positive thinking in promoting holistic health and the importance of adapting practices to different cultures.

Insights from Emotional Harmony:

- The Luminary of Emotional Harmony highlighted the impact of positive emotions on mental health and the role of creative expression in fostering emotional well-being.

Insights from Social Harmony:

- The Luminary of Social Harmony discussed how positive communication fosters community unity and the significance of inclusive events in celebrating diversity.

Insights from Environmental Harmony:

- The Luminary of Environmental Harmony emphasized the link between humanity and nature and the benefits of eco-conscious living.

7. Mastery of Harmony Techniques: The Luminary Showcase

With their insights shared, the Luminary leaders prepared for the Luminary Showcase, a celebration where each team demonstrated their mastery of harmony techniques.

In amphitheater, communities, skeptics, and supporters watched as the teams showcased their initiatives, illustrating the integration of physical, emotional, social, and environmental harmony.

8. Legacy: Spreading the Symphony Beyond the Library

As the showcase ended, Aria revealed the next phase of their journey. The Luminary leader, now masters of harmony techniques, would carry their teachings to new cities, facing unique challenges and spreading the power of positive thinking and cosmic harmony.

Fueled by their growth and insights, the Luminary leaders embraced this next chapter. Aria's parting words echoed, "Your journey continues, and the symphony of positive change will resonate in new places. The cosmic legacy is an eternal melody that harmonizes the universe."

The hidden library, now a sanctuary of wisdom, faded as the Luminary leaders set off on their next adventure, ready to spread the symphony of unity and balance far and wide.

Training in Harmony Techniques - Summary with Leadership Lessons

Chapter 4 of the book explores the transformative phase of Training in Harmony Techniques, where the Luminaries delve into the integration of positive thinking with specific strategies for fostering unity and balance. Here are management and leadership lessons derived from this chapter:

Visionary Leadership:

- Effective leaders guide their teams with a visionary perspective. Aria's cosmic vision sets the stage for the Luminary leaders, emphasizing the importance of aligning individual strengths with overarching goals to create a harmonious tapestry.

Strengths-Based Leadership:

- Leaders should recognize and leverage the unique strengths of each team member. The Luminary leaders engage in a strengths-based approach, aligning individuals with tasks that capitalize on their innate abilities and inclinations.

Purpose-Driven Team Formation:

- The Luminary leaders form teams with a clear purpose, aligning each team with specific realms of expertise. Purpose-driven teams foster a sense of belonging and dedication among team members, contributing to the overall success of the organization.

Holistic Development and Continuous Learning:

- The hidden library transforms into a training ground, emphasizing the importance of continuous learning. Leaders should provide opportunities for skill development and holistic training, fostering a culture of growth and adaptability within their teams.

Adaptability and Innovation:

- Leaders must guide their teams in adapting positive thinking techniques to unique challenges. The Luminary leaders demonstrate the importance of flexibility and innovation in overcoming obstacles and achieving transformative results.

Positive Communication Strategies:

- Leaders face scepticism and resistance, and effective communication is key. The Luminary leaders navigate scepticism by employing positive communication strategies, emphasizing evidence-based success stories, and dismantling barriers through open dialogue.

Resilience and Innovation in Leadership:

- The challenges faced by the Harmony Teams become opportunities for resilience and innovation. Leaders should instil a mindset of resilience, encouraging their teams to adapt and innovate in the face of adversity, reinforcing the transformative potential of positive thinking.

Celebration of Success:

- The Harmony Convergence Ritual and Luminary Showcase become celebrations of success. Leaders should create platforms to celebrate achievements, fostering a positive culture and inspiring teams to overcome future challenges.

Reflection and Continuous Improvement:

- Reflection is crucial for continuous improvement. Leaders, like the Luminary leaders reflecting on their journey, should encourage introspection within their teams, acknowledging successes, learning from challenges, and adapting strategies for ongoing growth.

Vision for Future Endeavours:

- Leaders should have a vision for the future, guiding their teams toward new horizons. Aria's Harmonic Vision represents the importance of long-term goals, inspiring teams to envision and work towards a future where positive change is a continuous journey.

In summary, Chapter 4 intertwines wisdom with practical management and leadership lessons. The Luminary leaders' training in harmony techniques emphasizes visionary leadership, strengths-based approaches, purpose-driven team formation, adaptability, positive communication, resilience, celebration of success, reflection, and a forward-looking vision. These lessons serve as a guiding light for leaders in the real world, fostering positive change, continuous improvement, and a harmonious workplace culture.

Initial Challenges and Adaptation & Cultural Integration

After the Harmony Convergence Ritual and Luminary Showcase, the Harmony Teams left the hidden library and ventured into various places—cities, villages, and urban centers—each with its own challenges and opportunities. Chapter 5, "Initial Challenges and Adaptation," describes how the Luminaries faced their first tests in these new environments.

1. The Luminary of Physical Harmony: Facing Skepticism About Well-being

In a busy city, the Luminary of Physical Harmony encountered skepticism about well-being practices. Convincing diverse communities of the benefits of holistic health was their first challenge.

Adapting to the Situation:

- The Luminary worked with local healthcare providers and conducted studies to show the positive effects of well-being practices on physical health. This approach provided concrete evidence and turned skepticism into curiosity.

Using New Skills:

- Positive thinking techniques were used in community workshops and demonstrations. The Luminary adapted these practices to fit different cultural contexts, showing that well-being is not a one-size-fits-all concept.

2. The Luminary of Emotional Harmony: Overcoming Stigmas with Art

In a peaceful village surrounded by nature, the Luminary of Emotional Harmony needed to break stigmas around mental health and promote artistic expression for emotional well-being.

Adapting to the Situation:

- The Luminary collaborated with local artists and psychologists to organize art workshops and create safe spaces for emotional dialogue. The approach was tailored to the village's culture, encouraging free expression of emotions.

Using New Skills:

- Affirmations for emotional resilience were included in the workshops. The Luminary showed the power of positive thinking by helping individuals embrace and express their emotions creatively.

3. The Luminary of Social Harmony: Bridging Divides in a Diverse Community

In a culturally diverse urban center, the Luminary of Social Harmony faced the challenge of bridging divides within the community. Initial resistance came from cultural differences and historical tensions.

Adapting to the Situation:

- The Luminary engaged with local leaders, organized town hall meetings, and started projects celebrating cultural diversity. Their adaptability was evident in their diplomatic approach and fostering open dialogues.

Using New Skills:

- Positive communication strategies were used to break down barriers and build unity. The Luminary demonstrated the potential of harmony by fostering understanding and inclusivity through community events.

4. The Luminary of Environmental Harmony: Promoting Eco-consciousness

In a town focused on sustainability, the Luminary of Environmental Harmony faced resistance to eco-conscious practices and needed to inspire sustainable living.

Adapting to the Situation:

- The Luminary started pilot projects, collaborated with local businesses, and engaged with schools to raise awareness about environmental well-being. Strategies were aligned with the town's existing eco-conscious efforts.

Using New Skills:

- Affirmations for eco-conscious living were part of educational campaigns. The Luminary emphasized the relationship between humanity and nature, turning skeptics into advocates for sustainability.

5. Collaboration: The Harmonic Team Reunion

As the Harmony Teams faced their initial challenges, they felt the need for a reunion to share insights and celebrate their adaptive strategies.

Sharing Insights:

- The Luminary leaders returned to the hidden library to share their experiences and lessons learned. They highlighted how positive thinking techniques and adaptive strategies helped them overcome challenges.

Collaboration Showcase:

- Aria organized a showcase where each team presented the results of their initiatives. The teams demonstrated the power of positive change in diverse environments.

6. Wisdom Shared: Reflection and Growth

After the reunion, the Luminary leaders reflected on their experiences, guided by Aria's wisdom. They shared their insights on the challenges they faced and the growth they experienced.

Insights Shared:

- **Physical Harmony:** The importance of community collaboration and adapting practices to different cultures.

- **Emotional Harmony:** The impact of positive emotions on mental health and the power of creative expression.

- **Social Harmony:** The role of positive communication in fostering unity and the significance of inclusive events.

- **Environmental Harmony:** The connection between humanity and nature and the benefits of sustainable living.

7. Legacy Unveiled: The Next Phase

Aria revealed the next phase of their journey—the Cosmic Legacy. The Luminary leaders, now adept at adaptation and positive change, would take their harmony techniques to new places and face new challenges.

Adapting to New Settings:

- The Luminary leaders embraced their mission with renewed determination, guided by Aria to new cities where their positive change could make an impact.

Continuing the Journey:

- Aria's final words reminded them that their journey was just beginning. They were ready to spread harmony and positive change far and wide.

As the hidden library faded, the Luminary leaders prepared for the next phase. Guided by Aria's wisdom, they were ready to continue their journey, spreading the symphony of harmony to new places, transforming communities, and creating a world where positive change thrived.

Initial Challenges and Adaptation & Cultural Integration: Summary with Leadership Lessons

Chapter 5 of the book explores the journey of the Harmony Teams as they face initial challenges in diverse environments and showcase their adaptability and application of newly acquired skills to overcome obstacles. Here are management and leadership lessons derived from this chapter:

1. Adaptive Leadership:

- Effective leaders adapt their strategies to diverse environments. The Luminary leaders showcase adaptive leadership by tailoring their approaches to address unique challenges in each realm, recognizing the importance of flexibility in leadership.

2. Resilience in the Face of Challenges:

- Leaders must be resilient in the face of challenges. The Luminary leaders demonstrate resilience by navigating skepticism, breaking stigmas, bridging divides, and overcoming resistance, showcasing the importance of perseverance and determination in leadership.

3. Cultural Sensitivity and Inclusivity:

- In diverse environments, cultural sensitivity and inclusivity are crucial. The Luminary leaders emphasize the importance of understanding and respecting cultural nuances, fostering an inclusive environment that promotes positive change.

4. Collaborative Leadership:

- Leaders should engage in collaborative leadership, fostering partnerships with local stakeholders, leaders, and experts. The Luminary leaders collaborate with local communities, healthcare providers, artists, psychologists, businesses, and educators, demonstrating the power of teamwork in achieving shared goals.

5. Application of Positive Thinking Techniques:

- Positive thinking techniques are powerful tools for leaders. The Luminary leaders integrate affirmations, positive communication, and resilience-building strategies into their initiatives, showcasing the transformative potential of a positive mindset in overcoming challenges.

6. Evidence-Based Leadership:

- Leaders should rely on evidence-based approaches. The Luminary leaders engage in research studies, educational campaigns, and community initiatives supported by evidence, reinforcing the importance of data-driven decision-making in leadership.

7. Community Engagement and Communication:

- Effective leaders engage with communities and prioritize open communication. The Luminary leaders organize town hall meetings, workshops, and events to foster dialogue, highlighting the significance of transparent and inclusive communication in leadership.

8. Sustainable Leadership Practices:

- Leaders should promote sustainability in their initiatives. The Luminary leaders initiate eco-conscious projects, sustainable living campaigns, and partnerships with local businesses, emphasizing the long-term impact of sustainable practices on community well-being.

9. Reflection and Continuous Improvement:

- Reflection is essential for continuous improvement. The Luminary leaders engage in a cosmic reflection, acknowledging insights, challenges, and growth. This emphasizes the importance of introspection and ongoing learning in effective leadership.

10. Visionary Leadership for Future Endeavours:

- Visionary leadership guides future endeavours. Aria unveils the Cosmic Legacy, emphasizing the Luminary leaders' role as cosmic architects of positive change. Leaders should have a long-term vision that inspires teams and propels them toward new horizons.

11. Adaptation as a Leadership Skill:

- Adaptation is a critical leadership skill. The Luminary leaders showcase their adaptability in different environments, demonstrating the importance of leaders being responsive to change and capable of adjusting strategies to fit evolving circumstances.

12. Celebration of Adaptive Success:

- Leaders should celebrate adaptive success. The Luminary Showcase becomes a celebration of achievements, reinforcing the positive culture within teams. Leaders should create platforms to acknowledge and appreciate the adaptive efforts of their teams.

In summary, Chapter 5 intertwines wisdom with practical management and leadership lessons. The Luminary leaders' journey of facing initial challenges and adapting to diverse environments highlights the importance of adaptive leadership, resilience, cultural sensitivity, collaborative approaches, evidence-based practices, community engagement, sustainability, reflection, visionary leadership, and forward-looking vision. These lessons serve as a guide for leaders in the real world, fostering positive change, continuous improvement, and adaptive leadership practices in the ever-evolving landscape of leadership.

Building Sustainable Alliances

The Harmony Teams, guided by the Luminary leaders, continued their journey across different worlds, focusing on forming lasting connections with local communities and organizations. This Chapter, "Building Sustainable Alliances," describes their efforts to create enduring partnerships that promote harmony.

1. The Luminary of Physical Harmony: Healing Partnerships for Community Well-being

The Luminary of Physical Harmony visited a town known for its holistic well-being practices. Their goal was to build sustainable partnerships with local healers, healthcare providers, and wellness practitioners to promote community health.

Building Sustainable Alliances:

- The Luminary talked with local healers to understand their practices and included these in new wellness initiatives. Partnerships with healthcare providers helped create accessible wellness programs, focusing on a united vision for community health.

Positive Collaboration:

- The town embraced holistic well-being practices, thanks to the collaboration between the Luminary, local healers, and healthcare providers. This partnership led to a lasting harmony that prioritized individual and community well-being.

2. The Luminary of Emotional Harmony: Empowering Artistic Alliances

In a city famous for its artistic expression, the Luminary of Emotional Harmony aimed to build sustainable alliances with local artists, psychologists, and cultural organizations. Their mission was to empower individuals through emotional well-being and artistic expression.

Building Sustainable Alliances:

- The Luminary worked with local artists to organize workshops and events that combined emotional well-being practices with artistic expression. They also partnered with psychologists to provide mental health support.

Positive Collaboration:

- The city saw a growth in emotional resilience and artistic expression. The Luminary's focus on sustainable alliances with local artists and psychologists created a lasting harmony that celebrated diverse emotional and artistic stories.

3. The Luminary of Social Harmony: Unity Through Community Partnerships

In a diverse urban center, the Luminary of Social Harmony focused on building sustainable alliances with community leaders, organizations, and activists to foster unity and bridge divides.

Building Sustainable Alliances:

- The Luminary talked with community leaders to understand their unique challenges and goals. They formed partnerships with local organizations to organize inclusive events and community-building projects.

Positive Collaboration:

- The city transformed as these sustainable alliances fostered unity and understanding. Collaboration with community leaders and organizations built a foundation for lasting harmony, breaking down barriers and creating a shared sense of identity.

4. The Luminary of Environmental Harmony: Eco-Conscious Alliances for Planetary Well-being

In a town dedicated to environmental stewardship, the Luminary of Environmental Harmony focused on building sustainable alliances with local environmentalists, businesses, and educational institutions to promote eco-conscious living.

Building Sustainable Alliances:

- The Luminary worked with local environmentalists on projects that supported the town's commitment to sustainability. They partnered with businesses to encourage eco-friendly practices and developed educational programs with schools.

Positive Collaboration:

- The town adopted a sustainable lifestyle, integrating eco-conscious practices into daily life. Collaborating with environmentalists, businesses, and educational institutions led to lasting harmony that connected humanity with the natural world.

5. Collaboration Showcase: Celebrating Sustainable Alliances

As the Harmony Teams built sustainable alliances, Aria organized a Collaboration Showcase to celebrate their achievements. The Luminary leaders and their teams gathered to present the positive outcomes of their partnerships.

Showcasing Positive Collaboration:

- Each Harmony Team shared the results of their alliances, highlighting stories of empowerment, unity, and planetary well-being. This event demonstrated the transformative power of positive collaboration.

Reflection on Sustainable Alliances:

- Aria guided the Luminary leaders in reflecting on their experiences. The showcased collaborations became a narrative of hope and inspiration, emphasizing the importance of sustainable alliances.

6. Insights Shared: Wisdom of Sustainable Alliances

After the showcase, the Luminary leaders shared insights from their experiences, recognizing the importance of fostering positive collaboration for lasting harmony.

Insights Shared:

- The Luminary of Physical Harmony valued the healing partnerships with local healers and healthcare providers, noting the importance of sustainable alliances in holistic community well-being.

- The Luminary of Emotional Harmony celebrated the empowerment through artistic alliances, highlighting the impact of collaborating with local artists and psychologists.

- The Luminary of Social Harmony emphasized the unity achieved through community partnerships, showing how alliances can break social barriers and create a shared identity.

- The Luminary of Environmental Harmony reflected on the town's eco-conscious living, stressing the role of sustainable alliances in harmonizing humanity and nature.

7. Legacy Unveiled: The Alliance Symphony Continues

Aria revealed the next phase of their journey: the Alliance Symphony. The Luminary leaders, now experts in building sustainable alliances, would continue to spread harmony to new realms, adapting their positive thinking techniques to strengthen alliances.

Harmony in Diverse Settings:

- The Luminary leaders, guided by Aria, set out to new cities where positive change awaited. Building sustainable alliances would remain an ongoing effort, creating lasting harmony in every place they touched.

Eternal Melody of Alliance Harmony:

- Aria's final words reminded them that their journey of forming alliances was a continuous process. The legacy of these alliances would resonate through the universe, creating an enduring harmony.

8. The Alliance Dance Continues: An Everlasting Harmony

As the echoes of the Cosmic Collaboration Showcase faded, the Luminary leaders prepared for the next phase. Their journey, fueled by the power of sustainable alliances, would continue to impact diverse realms.

Aria's guidance remained a beacon as they ventured into new horizons. The hidden library, once a sanctuary of wisdom, had become the starting point for their cosmic journey. The alliances and positive thinking techniques they mastered would create an enduring universe.

With the hidden library behind them, the Luminary leaders embraced their roles as architects of harmony. The symphony of sustainable alliances would continue to transform communities, foster unity, and create a world where positive change endured. The Luminary leaders, driven by cosmic wisdom and positive thinking, were ready to spread this harmony far and wide.

Building Sustainable Alliances – Summary with Management/Leadership Lessons

This Chapter of the book," "Building Sustainable Alliances," shows how the Luminary leaders and their teams create lasting partnerships with local communities and organizations. Here are the key leadership and management lessons:

1. **Visionary Leadership in Alliance Building:**

- Effective leaders need a clear vision for positive collaboration, aligning with the values of local communities to create lasting harmony.

2. **Adaptive Leadership for Sustainable Initiatives:**

- Leaders must adapt their strategies to meet the unique needs of different communities, ensuring the longevity of positive collaboration.

3. **Collaborative Leadership for Unity:**

- Leaders should prioritize teamwork, engaging in dialogue and partnerships with local stakeholders to achieve shared goals and foster community unity.

4. **Cultural Intelligence in Alliance Formation:**

- Understanding and respecting diverse cultural perspectives is crucial for successful alliance building. Leaders should incorporate cultural nuances into their initiatives.

5. **Positive Communication for Lasting Impact:**

- Effective leaders use positive communication strategies that bridge cultural and organizational differences, helping to build lasting positive collaborations.

In summary, this Chapter highlights the importance of visionary, adaptive, and collaborative leadership in building sustainable alliances. These lessons emphasize the need for cultural intelligence and positive communication to create enduring harmony through collaboration with local communities and organizations. These principles are valuable for leaders aiming to make a positive impact in diverse and interconnected environments.

Navigating Environmental Challenges

The Harmony Teams, guided by the Luminary leaders, found themselves in various places facing unique environmental problems. Chapter on, "Navigating Environmental Challenges," tells their journey as they encounter these obstacles and find creative solutions. This chapter focuses on the positive mindset needed to tackle and overcome these challenges, highlighting resilience, adaptability, and the power of positive thinking.

1. The Luminary of Physical Harmony: Healing in a Fragile Ecosystem

The Luminary of Physical Harmony led the team to a delicate ecosystem suffering from environmental damage. Their task was to restore balance and health to this struggling habitat.

- **Facing Environmental Challenges:**

- The Luminary worked with local communities, scientists, and environmentalists to understand the causes of damage, such as deforestation, pollution, and habitat loss. They needed new solutions to heal the ecosystem and promote physical harmony.

- **Positive Mindset in Action:**

- Embracing a positive attitude, the Luminary encouraged the team to see challenges as opportunities.

They focused on community engagement, tree-planting initiatives, and sustainable practices to restore the ecosystem. This positive mindset helped them stay resilient in tough times.

2. **The Luminary of Emotional Harmony: Building Resilience in a Climate-Affected City**

In a city dealing with climate change impacts, the Luminary of Emotional Harmony aimed to build resilience in the face of environmental uncertainty.

- **Facing Environmental Challenges:**

- The Luminary saw rising sea levels, extreme weather, and the emotional strain on residents. Emotional Harmony was crucial for addressing these issues, requiring new approaches to build resilience and foster a positive mindset in the community.

- **Positive Mindset in Action:**

- The Luminary started emotional well-being programs, community support networks, and climate resilience workshops. They infused a positive attitude into the city, helping residents adapt to environmental changes. This approach showed the power of positive thinking in overcoming emotional challenges.

3. The Luminary of Social Harmony: Uniting a Resource-Scarce Region

In a region facing resource scarcity and social divides, the Luminary of Social Harmony worked to promote unity and sustainable resource management.

- **Facing Environmental Challenges:**

- The Luminary addressed conflicts over scarce resources, emphasizing the need for fair distribution and teamwork. Issues included water shortages, land disputes, and economic inequalities. They sought new ways to bridge divides and promote social and environmental harmony.

- **Positive Mindset in Action:**

- The Luminary encouraged a positive attitude, focusing on shared solutions instead of problems. They organized community discussions, sustainable resource management projects, and economic empowerment programs. This positive mindset helped break down barriers and build a united front against environmental challenges.

4. The Luminary of Environmental Harmony: Preserving Biodiversity in a Threatened Sanctuary

In a sanctuary rich in biodiversity but threatened by habitat destruction, the Luminary of Environmental Harmony aimed to preserve this delicate balance.

- **Facing Environmental Challenges:**

- The Luminary saw the effects of deforestation, poaching, and habitat fragmentation on the sanctuary's species. They needed to restore habitats, protect wildlife, and involve the community. They looked for innovative ways to ensure the sanctuary's survival.

- **Positive Mindset in Action:**

- The Luminary promoted a positive attitude, seeing challenges as conservation opportunities. They worked with local communities, introduced sustainable tourism, and started educational programs. This positive mindset helped create a sanctuary where biodiversity could thrive.

5. **Collaboration: Sharing Innovations and Insights**

As the Harmony Teams tackled environmental challenges, Aria organized a Cosmic Collaboration Symposium where Luminary leaders and their teams could share their solutions and insights.

- **Showcasing Innovations:**

- Each team presented their solutions to environmental challenges, highlighting the positive mindset guiding their actions. They showcased sustainable practices and community engagement initiatives, demonstrating positive change.

- **Insights Shared:**

- Aria led a reflection session, acknowledging the lessons learned from these challenges. The positive mindset shown in the forum became a source of hope and inspiration.

6. **Insights Shared: Cosmic Wisdom on Environmental Harmony**

After the showcase, the Luminary leaders shared their insights from navigating environmental challenges, recognizing the importance of a positive mindset for environmental harmony.

- **Insights Shared:**

- The Luminary of Physical Harmony spoke about the power of positive thinking in healing ecosystems, emphasizing community-led restoration efforts.

- The Luminary of Emotional Harmony discussed building resilience through emotional well-being programs.

- The Luminary of Social Harmony highlighted the role of a positive mindset in overcoming social divides and promoting sustainable resource management.

- The Luminary of Environmental Harmony reflected on how viewing challenges as opportunities led to successful biodiversity conservation.

7. Aria's Guidance: The Environmental Symphony Continues

Aria introduced the next phase of their journey—the Environmental Symphony. Her guidance served as a compass, directing the Luminary leaders to new places where they could continue to find innovative solutions and maintain a positive mindset.

- **Harmony in Diversity:**
- The Luminary leaders embraced the Environmental Symphony with renewed determination, encouraged by Aria's wisdom. They prepared to explore new areas, continuing their efforts to create lasting harmony.

- **Eternal Melody of Environmental Harmony:**
- Aria's final words reminded them, "The Environmental Symphony is an ongoing journey—a harmonious exploration of new solutions and a positive mindset. Your work continues, and the harmony you create will resonate throughout the universe."

8. The Symphony Resonates: Creating Everlasting Harmony

As the hidden library echoed with the Environmental Symphony, the Luminary leaders prepared for the next phase of their journey. The combination of innovative solutions and a positive mindset fueled their ongoing efforts.

- **Journey Continues:**
- Guided by Aria, the Luminary leaders moved forward, ready to spread environmental harmony. The hidden library, once a place of ancient wisdom, had become the starting point for a cosmic journey of lasting impact.

As the hidden library faded from view, the Luminary leaders, now architects of environmental harmony, embraced their next challenges. Their efforts would continue to transform habitats, promote unity, and create a world where positive change persisted. The Luminary leaders, driven by wisdom and a positive mindset, were ready to spread environmental harmony far and wide.

Navigating Environmental Challenges – Leadership and Management Lessons

"Navigating Environmental Challenges," shows how the Harmony Teams handle unique environmental issues. Here are the key leadership and management lessons from the Luminary leaders' experiences:

1. **Embracing Innovation in Problem-Solving:**

- Leaders need to embrace innovation when facing environmental challenges. Creative problem-solving and exploring unique solutions tailored to each problem are crucial. Encourage a culture of innovation, fostering adaptability and resourcefulness within teams.

2. **Fostering a Positive Mindset in Adversity:**

- The Luminary leaders show the power of a positive mindset when dealing with environmental challenges. Cultivate resilience and inspire teams to see opportunities in difficulties. Prioritize and nurture a positive attitude, fostering an optimistic and solution-oriented culture.

3. **Collaborative Approaches for Sustainable Solutions:**

- Collaboration is key in addressing environmental challenges. Engage with local communities, scientists, and experts, emphasizing collective efforts. Foster collaboration within teams, recognizing that diverse perspectives lead to more sustainable solutions.

4. **Adaptive Leadership for Changing Environments:**

- Adapt leadership approaches to address the unique challenges of each setting. A one-size-fits-all strategy is insufficient. Learn the importance of adaptability, adjusting strategies to suit the dynamic nature of business environments.

5. **Communicating a Vision of Environmental Harmony:**

- Effective communication of a vision for environmental harmony inspires teams and communities to work toward a common goal. Use the power of communication to foster a shared sense of purpose, aligning individuals toward collective positive change.

In summary, Chapter 9 provides practical guidance for leaders and managers, emphasizing the importance of innovation, a positive mindset, collaboration, adaptability, and effective communication when facing environmental challenges. These principles contribute to the success of environmental efforts and offer valuable lessons for leading teams and organizations toward positive change.

Climax - The Symphony of Harmony

In the journey of positive change, the Luminary leaders and their Harmony Teams reached a big moment—the Symphony of Harmony. Chapter 10 unfolds as a grand event where the Luminaries showcase their efforts in bringing harmony to different places. The symphony celebrates unity and positive change, echoing across the universe and leaving a lasting impact on communities.

1. **Prelude to the Symphony: Getting Ready**

Before the Symphony of Harmony, Aria helped the Luminary leaders and their teams prepare. The hidden library turned into a stage for the event, glowing with energy. They worked on cultural exchanges and environmental exhibits, creating an immersive experience reflecting their diverse journey.

- **Reflections:**

- Aria encouraged the Luminaries to think back on their journey, realizing how positive thinking and harmony transformed different places. These reflections set the stage for the grand Symphony of Harmony.

2. **Act I: Celebrating Cultural Harmony**

The symphony started with Act I, focusing on the cultural harmony created by the Luminaries. Each Harmony Team showed how they bridged cultural gaps through traditional performances and interactive displays, fostering unity.

Communities touched by these initiatives shared stories of understanding, collaboration, and newfound friendships. They celebrated shared traditions and a sense of belonging beyond borders.

3. Act II: The Environmental Symphony

Next was Act II—the Environmental Symphony. The Luminary leaders presented their solutions for healing ecosystems, building resilience to climate change, and protecting biodiversity. The stage lit up with examples of positive change in the environment.

Communities facing environmental challenges thanked the Harmony Teams for their help. They saw improved habitats, sustainable practices, and a commitment to protecting nature.

4. Act III: Social Harmony in Action

Act III focused on social initiatives. The Luminary leaders showcased projects aimed at breaking down social barriers and promoting fair resource distribution, creating narratives of unity and empowerment.

Communities once divided celebrated their transformations. They now shared resources, had economic opportunities, and stronger bonds. Prosperity and peace became the new norm.

5. **Act IV: Individual Growth**

As the symphony reached its peak, Act IV highlighted individual growth and the power of positive thinking. The stage reflected personal transformations and the role individuals played in creating positive change.

Communities saw how individual changes led to resilience and empowerment. People became leaders in their communities, spreading positivity and inspiring others.

6. **Finale: A Celebration**

As the Symphony of Harmony ended, the audience from across the universe cheered. Aria, the Luminary leaders, and their teams felt proud of their achievements. The symphony's impact would be felt for ages, creating a legacy of positive change.

Aria's last words echoed, "The Symphony of Harmony is a timeless celebration of unity and positivity. Your journey continues, shaping the destiny of the universe."

Climax - The Symphony of Harmony – Leadership and Management Lessons

This Chapter shows the culmination of the Luminaries' journey and offers valuable lessons:

1. **Celebrating Diversity and Unity:**

- Leaders should celebrate diversity and foster unity among teams and communities to achieve shared goals.

2. **Transformative Power of Positive Impact:**

- Positive thinking leads to tangible and lasting change, creating a ripple effect that impacts individuals and communities.

3. **Showcasing Achievements Through Communication:**

- Effective communication highlights achievements and fosters engagement and support.

4. **Legacy Building Through Enduring Impact:**

- Focus on initiatives that leave a lasting, positive impact on organizations and communities.

5. **Guiding Teams Toward a Shared Vision:**

- Provide clear guidance and align teams toward a shared purpose for collective success.

In summary, this Chapter celebrates the transformative power of positive thinking and unity, leaving a lasting impact on the universe. As the hidden library disappeared, the Luminary leaders embarked on their next cosmic adventure, ready to shape the destiny of the universe.

Conclusion: Embracing Positive Transformation

Thank you for joining us on this journey through the pages of "How to Embrace Positive Transformation." As you turn the final page, we hope you feel inspired and empowered to embark on your own path of positive change.

Throughout the chapters, we've explored various aspects of transformation, from facing new challenges to building sustainable alliances and navigating environmental obstacles. Each chapter has offered valuable insights and practical techniques to help you embrace positive transformation in your life and community.

As you reflect on the lessons learned and the techniques practiced, remember that knowledge alone is not enough. True transformation comes from action—implementing what you've learned and integrating it into your daily life.

It's essential to recognize that change is not always easy. There will be challenges and moments of uncertainty along the way. But it's in these moments that we have the opportunity to grow and evolve.

So, we encourage you to practice the techniques you've learned, whether it's fostering harmony in your relationships, promoting sustainability in your community, or cultivating internal peace and well-being.

Remember, small steps lead to significant change. By taking consistent action and remaining open to new possibilities, you can create a ripple effect of positivity and transformation in your life and the lives of those around you.

Thank you for allowing us to be a part of your journey toward positive transformation. May you continue to embrace the power of harmony, unity, and positivity as you navigate the ever-changing landscape of life.

Wishing you joy, fulfilment, and boundless opportunities for growth on your journey ahead.

Disclaimer

This book is for entertainment purposes only. Readers acknowledge that the author does not render legal, financial, medical, or professional advice. The content within this book has been derived from various sources. Please consult a licensed professional before attempting any techniques outlined in this book.

By reading this document, the reader agrees that under no circumstances is the author responsible for any direct or indirect losses incurred as a result of the use of the information contained within this document, including but not limited to errors, omissions, or inaccuracies. Adherence to all applicable laws and regulations, including international, federal, state, and local governing professional licensing, business practices, advertising, and all other jurisdictions, is the sole responsibility of the purchaser or reader. Neither the author nor the publisher assumes any responsibility or liability whatsoever on behalf of the purchaser or reader of these materials. Any perceived slight of any individual or organization is purely unintentional.

About the Author

Mahuya Gupta (B.Sc, B.Tech, M.Sc Engg, MBA), the author of "Secrets to Leverage The Power of Focus," is a dynamic professional whose career has traversed diverse realms. With a background in Applied Physics and Engineering, she honed her skills in the corporate arena, progressing from an entry-level position to a senior management role within a renowned multinational corporation in India.

A passion for writing kindled in her school days has always burned brightly within her, earning the admiration of her teachers. Although this creative pursuit took a backseat during her higher education and corporate journey, it is now rekindled with vigor through this book.

Mahuya's writing is informed by extensive research and a wealth of knowledge accumulated over her 20+ years in the corporate world. Beyond her literary endeavors, Mahuya is a multi-talented artist, proficient in various mediums of painting and a skilled violinist, with a trove of accolades garnered during her academic journey.

She can be contacted at authormahuya@gmail.com, inviting readers to engage in meaningful conversations about focus, creativity, and her diverse passions.

May I Ask You For A Small Favor?

First, I want to thank you for taking the time to read this book. You could have chosen any other book, but you took mine, and I totally appreciate this.

I hope you got at least a few actionable insights that will have a positive impact on your day-to-day life.

Can I ask for 30 seconds more of your time?

I'd love it if you could leave a review about the book. Reviews may not matter to big-name authors, but they're a tremendous help for authors like me, who don't have much following. They help me to grow my readership by encouraging folks to take a chance on my books.

To put it straight - reviews are the lifeblood of any author. Kindly visit the store where you bought this book to provide your valuable review. It will just take less than a minute of your time, but it will tremendously help me to reach out to more people, so please leave your review. Thanks for your support of my work. And I'd love to see your review.

Other Books Written By The Author

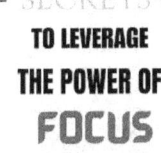

Click here to buy   **Click here to buy**

www.ingramcontent.com/pod-product-compliance
Lightning Source LLC
Chambersburg PA
CBHW052334220526
45472CB00001B/421